TRADITIONS AND CELEBRATIONS

NEW YEAR

by Charles C. Hofer

PEBBLE
a capstone imprint

Published by Pebble, an imprint of Capstone
1710 Roe Crest Drive
North Mankato, Minnesota 56003
capstonepub.com

Copyright © 2024 by Capstone. All rights reserved. No part of this publication may be reproduced in whole or in part, or stored in a retrieval system, or transmitted in any form or by any means, electronic, mechanical, photocopying, recording, or otherwise, without written permission of the publisher.

Library of Congress Cataloging-in-Publication Data is available on the Library of Congress website.
ISBN: 9780756575816 (library binding)
ISBN: 9780756575762 (paperback)
ISBN: 9780756575779 (ebook PDF)

Summary: People all over the world celebrate the New Year. It's a holiday that celebrates new beginnings and the hope for a successful year ahead. People love gathering at parties to greet the New Year with fireworks, music, and more. Learn the many ways people count down the final moments of the old year and celebrate the birth of a brand new year.

Editorial Credits
Editor: Aaron Sautter; Designer: Jaime Willems; Media Researcher: Rebekah Hubstenberger; Production Specialist: Whitney Schaefer

Photo Credits
Alamy: Chronicle, 8, ZUMA Press, Inc., 14; Getty Images: Ezra Acayan, 26, Jose Luis Pelaez, 11, Jupiterimages, 25, kate_sept2004, 21, Klaus Vedfelt, 13, martin-dm, 1, Martina Unbehauen, 24, ozgurcankaya, 22, Priscila Zambotto, 29, skynesher, 16, SolStock, 12; Shutterstock: Betty Shelton, 23, GreenArt, 18, kwanchai.c, 20, Linda Hughes Photography, 19, Milleflore Images, 7, Natalya Mok, 6, ROBERTO ZILLI, 17, Standret, cover, Yuganov Konstantin, 5

Design Elements
Shutterstock: Rafal Kulik

All internet sites appearing in back matter were available and accurate when this book was sent to press.

Printed and bound in China. PO5379

TABLE OF CONTENTS

HAPPY NEW YEAR! 4

NEW YEAR'S EVE 10

NEW YEAR'S DAY 16

NEW YEAR AROUND
THE WORLD 22

GLOSSARY 30

READ MORE 31

INTERNET SITES 31

INDEX 32

ABOUT THE AUTHOR 32

Words in **bold** are in the glossary.

HAPPY NEW YEAR!

It's almost **midnight**. Everyone's dressed up in fancy clothes. It's a big party. Tasty food is being served. People wait for fireworks to light up the sky. They count down the seconds: three, two, one . . . happy New Year!

The New Year is an important holiday around the world. It's a time to celebrate with family and friends. People enjoy good food and fun **traditions**. A brand new year is here!

In the United States, the New Year is celebrated over two days. New Year's Eve is December 31. This is the last day of the year. New Year's Day is celebrated the next day on January 1.

The New Year is a special time. It's a time to look back and remember the past year. New Year's is also a time to look toward the future. What will the New Year bring?

Ancient people were given mistletoe to celebrate the new year.

People have celebrated the New Year for thousands of years. Some **cultures** once celebrated the holiday at different times of year. It depended on which **calendar** they used.

Today, most countries use the Gregorian calendar. It's been used since 1582. For those countries, the New Year starts on January 1.

NEW YEAR'S EVE

New Year celebrations begin on New Year's Eve. It's December 31, the last day of the year. There are a lot of fun things to do on New Year's Eve.

Big parties take place on New Year's Eve. Some people wear fancy clothes. People like to stay up late to count down to the New Year. They get ready to say goodbye to the old year and ring in the new one.

On New Year's Eve, family and friends often gather for smaller parties. They might wear funny hats and use loud **noisemakers**.

A big tradition is counting down to the New Year. They count down the final seconds on the clock. At the stroke of midnight, people shout, "Happy New Year!"

People often touch their drinking glasses when making a toast.

At that moment, lots of things happen. People cheer and throw **confetti**. Some people light fireworks. Others might give a **toast** to wish each other good health.

2020 New Year's Eve ball drop in New York City

Another New Year's Eve tradition is the ball drop. Thousands of people gather in New York City for this event. A giant glowing ball is lowered as the clock moves toward midnight. When the ball reaches the New Year sign, confetti fills the air. Fireworks light up the sky. Happy New Year!

Many other U.S. cities have similar traditions. In Atlanta, Georgia, they drop a giant peach. In Boise, Idaho, they drop a big potato. Nothing is too wacky to celebrate New Year's Eve.

NEW YEAR'S DAY

New Year's Day is very different than New Year's Eve. The party is over. Now it's time to eat good food. It's time to watch sports like football and ice hockey. It's January 1st. It's a brand new year!

Polar Plunge in Turin, Italy

New Year's Day is also full of traditions. Some are fun and zany. One is the Polar Plunge. Daring people put on swimsuits and jump into frozen lakes. That's cold! It's a wacky way to start the New Year.

Fruit-filled pannetone cake is popular on New Year's Day.

Food is a big part of New Year's Day too. Some foods are thought to bring good luck. Many people like to start off the New Year with a little luck.

Some people believe eating black-eyed peas brings good luck and health. Eating greens may bring wealth too. New Year's Day is a time to eat lots of good food. It's all good luck!

Black-eyed peas with greens

New Year's Day can be very special to some people. The holiday is the **symbol** of a new beginning. People can say goodbye to difficult times from the old year. With the New Year, they can start over.

Some people make New Year's **resolutions**. These are promises people make to themselves. Kids might decide to keep their room clean. Some people may decide to lose weight or to run a **marathon**. Others may choose to stop bad habits. The New Year brings many new possibilities.

NEW YEAR AROUND THE WORLD

Many cultures around the world have fun New Year traditions. In Spain, people eat 12 grapes at midnight. Each grape symbolizes one month of the year. Eating all 12 grapes means a good year is coming.

In Greece, people hang onions by their doors. Onions are a symbol of growth and rebirth in Greek homes. People believe the onions will help bring success in the New Year.

Eating tasty foods is another common New Year tradition. In Germany, people give out sweet candy treats shaped like pigs. These cute piggies are meant to bring good luck in the New Year.

In Mexico, people make homemade tamales to give to family and loved ones. This is a traditional food in Mexico. The warm tamales are thought to bring good luck for the New Year.

Fireworks on New Year's Eve in Manila, Philippines

Not all New Year traditions include food. People in the Philippines open all their windows on New Year's Eve. They believe that this helps welcome in the New Year.

In India, people burn a wooden statue of an old man. The statue is a symbol for the old year. Burning the statue makes way for the New Year to begin.

In some countries, the New Year is a time to get outside. January 1 is summertime in Brazil. People like to go to the beach. But in Canada, it's wintertime. It's freezing outside. Canadians often go ice fishing.

The New Year holiday is a fun time of year. It's a great time to celebrate with family and friends. No matter where you live, it's always fun to ring in the New Year.

New Year's Eve fireworks at the beach in Brazil

GLOSSARY

calendar (KAL-uhn-duhr)—a chart that shows the days, weeks, and months in a year

confetti (kuhn-FEH-tee)—small pieces of colored paper that people throw at parties, parades, and other celebrations

culture (KUHL-chuhr)—the way of life, ideas, customs, and traditions of a group of people

marathon (MAYR-uh-thon)—a long-distance race, usually covering 26.2 miles (42.2 kilometers)

midnight (MID-nite)—twelve o'clock in the middle of the night

noisemaker (NOYZ-may-kuhr)—a device used to make loud noises, usually at a party or celebration

resolution (rez-uh-LOO-shuhn)—a promise to yourself that you will try to do something new or different

symbol (SIM-buhl)—something, such as an object or special occasion, that represents something else

toast (TOHST)—to say something and take a drink to honor someone or wish them good health

tradition (truh-DISH-uhn)—a custom, idea, or belief passed down through time

READ MORE

Cooper, Sharon Katz. *Chinese New Year*. North Mankato, MN: Pebble, 2021.

Malaspina, Ann. *New Year Traditions Around the World*. Mankato, MN: The Child's World, 2022.

McGinty, Alice B. *Feasts and Festivals Around the World: From Lunar New Year to Christmas*. New York: Little Bee Books, 2022.

INTERNET SITES

Britannica Kids: New Year's Day
kids.britannica.com/kids/article/New-Years-Day/353529

January 01: New Year's Day
web-holidays.com/blog/1997/11/29/january-1-new-years-day

NatGeo Kids: Winter Celebrations
kids.nationalgeographic.com/pages/topic/winter-celebrations

INDEX

ball drop, 14, 15

calendars, 9
clothes, 4, 10
confetti, 13, 15
countdowns, 4, 10, 12

family, 4, 32, 12, 28
fireworks, 4, 13, 15, 26, 29
food, 4, 16, 18–19, 22, 23, 24–25
friends, 4, 12, 28

good luck, 18–19, 24, 25

midnight, 4, 12, 15, 22
mistletoe, 8

new beginnings, 7, 20–21, 23, 27
New Year's Day, 6, 8, 16–20
New Year's Eve, 6, 10, 12–13, 14, 15, 16, 26, 27, 29
noisemakers, 12

parties, 4, 10, 12, 16
Polar Plunge, 17

resolutions, 21

sports, 16
symbols, 20, 22, 23, 27

toasts, 13
traditions around the world, 15, 22–25, 26, 27, 28, 29

ABOUT THE AUTHOR

Charles C. Hofer enjoys writing books for young students. He's written many books about animals, culture, science, and sports for young readers to enjoy. Charles lives in Tucson, Arizona.